I. Introduction

In the early theoretical industrial organization literature, a variety of practices were seen as means to allow incumbents to increase or retain their market power. For example, Sylos Labini argued that by charging a price below the monopoly price (the "limit price") a monopolist can make entry seem less profitable. Other analyses took analogous views of practices like tying, vertical integration, and predatory pricing. These models were criticized in the 1960s and 1970s by individuals now identified with the "Chicago school." Using modern parlance, these critics noted that the proposed methods did not comprise perfect equilibria. For example, Stigler (1968 at 20) argued that what is relevant to the entrant is the post-entry price, no obvious functional relationship exists between that price and the pre-entry pricing decisions of the incumbent.

More recently, a literature has developed to identify conditions under which the earlier theoretical work can be valid. For example, Spence (1977) showed that an incumbent can invest in capacity that results in a low post-entry equilibrium price, and hence reduces the profitability of entry.[1] This recent work can be characterized as showing that certain actions can have *strategic commitment* value. In this context, commitment means that a firm makes some irreversible decision that changes the optimal reaction of the decision-maker. Strategic means that the decision is communicated to some other actor, with the intention of altering that actor's behavior. Both aspects are relevant to the equilibrium ultimately achieved. Absent commitment, any claims regarding future behavior are not credible. Absent communication, the commitment will not have its desired effect.

One branch of this recent literature focuses on the strategic value of vertical restraints. A contract or restraint is viewed as having strategic value if it is "observable." It has been argued that vertical

---

[1] This result, as well as the Stigler critique, was implicitly suggested by Pashigian (1968).

integration, tying, resale price maintenance (RPM), exclusive dealing and exclusive territory clauses[2] can all serve as "facilitating devices"—i.e., as means of extracting consumer surplus without necessarily serving to impede entry.[3] This contrasts with an earlier view that any surplus extractable through a vertical restraint can be extracted using a two-part tariff, indicating that vertical contracts must serve some other purpose. The key point of departure for this new branch of the literature is to relax the assumption of full information. In a multilateral setting, absent observability, the manufacturer has an incentive to offer bilateral contracts that opportunistically reduce other retailers' profits. The potential for opportunistic behavior prevents the manufacturer from using the set of two-part tariffs that maximize its profits. It follows that if vertical restraint contracts are observable in circumstances where two-part tariffs are not, they may enable manufacturers to achieve increased profits and consumer surplus extraction. This has raised questions about the appropriate status of these restraints under the law.

This paper confronts the conjecture that, by virtue of their observability, vertical contracts dominate two-part tariffs as means of extracting surplus from downstream purchasers. It may be realistic to view restraints such as RPM and exclusive territories as sufficiently public to be called observable in cases where two-part tariffs are not.[4] However, this is not sufficient to make them facilitating devices. To support a facilitating-device equilibrium, a vertical contract must be a strategic commitment. Contracts that are observable satisfy this property only if they involve irreversible action; observability is not enough. The

---

[2] On vertical integration, see Ordover, Salop, and Saloner (1990) or Hart and Tirole (1991); on tying, see Whinston (1990); on RPM see Shaffer (1991), and O'Brien and Shaffer (1992); on exclusive dealing see Mathewson and Winter (1987); on exclusive territories see Hart and Tirole (1991), O'Brien and Shaffer (1992) and McAfee and Schwartz (1991).

[3] In the antitrust literature, the expression, "facilitating device," has been used in reference to practices that facilitate collusion among firms. Its usage in this paper encompasses the facilitation of price increases in the absence of explicit collusion.

[4] The practical relevance of the observability assumption can depend on the legal regime, as we explain later in the paper. For example, a law that binds all parties to terms of contract signed by any one party will be effective only if it has provisions that make agreed terms sufficiently public.

main contribution of this paper is to highlight enforceability as a companion to observability among assumptions that must be met for a vertical contract to be a facilitating device in equilibrium, and to demonstrate the practical relevance of this point. As we show, the strategic *commitment* values of certain vertical contracts depend on what legal rules are applied by the courts. Contrary to conjectures found in the recent literature, evidence from the case law suggests that minimum RPM has not met the enforceability conditions necessary for it to be a strategic commitment. Nor in many instances have the exclusive territory contracts brought before the courts. Hence, the evidence suggests these vertical contracts have not met conditions necessary for them to be facilitating devices as portrayed in the recent literature.

To focus on conjectures from the recent literature, we accept certain premises about the bargaining environment and the manufacturer's incentive to contract. A key assumption we retain is that the interaction between the manufacturer and its distributors occurs in a static game. In such an environment, the manufacturer's prospect of future loss from post-contractual opportunism is minimal. For this reason, the assumption that the interaction occurs in a static game magnifies the potential for opportunism. In contrast, Klein and Murphy (1988) use a repeat-game model to show that RPM contracts can serve as a means to reduce retailer opportunism.

Other models of RPM use a static framework, but address motives for its use that are quite different from the one considered in this paper. For example, RPM (and, by implication, nonprice vertical restraint) has been seen as a means of ensuring retailer performance (Telser (1960)), of utilizing asymmetric information (Rey and Tirole (1986)), and of reducing cartel monitoring costs (see Overstreet (1983) for a review of collusive theories). To the extent our analysis casts doubt on conjectures from the recent literature, it suggests renewed interest in these alternatives and their underlying premises.

II. The Canonical Setting

A simple model is provided to clarify conditions under which vertical contracts have been viewed as sufficient to extract surplus[5] when two-part tariffs are not. A monopolist manufacturer sells its product through two retailers, A and B, who are presented with contracts on a take-it-or-leave-it basis. We focus initially on the two-part tariff contract, which consists of a wholesale price, W, and a lump-sum fee, F. We assume that retailers are differentiated from the customer perspective yet sell substitute products using identical, fixed-proportion technologies. In particular, a retailer must purchase a unit of the manufacturer's product (input) for every unit of output he sells. Retailers face demand functions with the standard properties, $Q_i = Q_i(P_i, P_j)$, $\partial Q_i/\partial P_i < 0$ and $|\partial Q_i/\partial P_i| > |\partial Q_j/\partial P_i|$. Let P_i^R be retailer i's unconstrained optimal price. We assume a reaction function with the property, $\partial P_i^R/\partial P_j > 0$. Finally, we assume that the manufacturer has a constant marginal cost, m, while retailers face a constant marginal cost equal to the cost of reselling the product, r, plus the wholesale price.

A static three-stage game characterizes the interaction between manufacturer and retailers. In the first stage, the manufacturer simultaneously offers terms of contract—W and F—to each retailer. Retailers independently decide whether to accept those terms in stage two. In stage three, the retailers compete, setting price in light of what they know about W and F. It is within this framework that the two-part tariff as a means of extracting downstream surplus has fallen under attack.[6]

The old view—that it would be impossible for any other vertical contract to improve on the two-part tariff as a means of extracting surplus from downstream—was based on the observation that there exists

---

[5] The general term, "surplus," is employed here to refer to differences between revenue and cost. More refined terminology, such as that used in distinguishing between economic rents and quasi-rents, tends not to be found in the facilitating-device literature on vertical restraints and is not necessary to accomplish the main objectives of this paper.

[6] See Hart and Tirole (1991), O'Brien and Shaffer (1992), and McAfee and Schwartz (1991).

an optimal retail price schedule, $\mathbf{P}^* = (P_A^*, P_B^*)$, at which profits of the manufacturer and retailers are jointly maximized and a related wholesale price, $\mathbf{W}^* = (W_A^*, W_B^*)$, at which retailers will choose those prices. Given the ability to make a take-it-or-leave-it offer, the manufacturer can choose a fixed fee, $\mathbf{F}^* = (F_A^*, F_B^*)$, sufficient to capture the joint profit.[7] The two-part tariff, $(\mathbf{W}^*, \mathbf{F}^*)$, is thus optimal from the manufacturer's perspective; through no other contract can additional surplus be extracted.[8]

The new view of two-part tariffs confronts the old with the observation that *once retailer A has paid the fixed fee,* F_A^*, the manufacturer's incentive is to depart from the "optimal" two-part tariff, $(\mathbf{W}^*, \mathbf{F}^*)$, by reducing retailer B's wholesale price and increasing his fixed fee. While this departure from the optimal contract can leave retailer B indifferent, retailer A is made worse off for having agreed to its terms. That is, lowering W_B leads retailer B to cut his price. Retailer B becomes willing to pay a higher fee, F_B^*, while retailer A's profit declines, falling below the fee, F_A^*, already paid. Given that retailer A can rationally anticipate this outcome, the manufacturer's optimal two-part tariff, $(\mathbf{W}^*, \mathbf{F}^*)$, is not an equilibrium. Absent observability, equilibrium is achieved where $W_A = W_B = m$, with a fee sufficient for the manufacturer to claim the joint profit, which is less than what is achieved at $(\mathbf{W}^*, \mathbf{F}^*)$.[9] It follows that vertical contracts without this defect of the two-part tariff may be superior means of extracting surplus from downstream.

The defect of the two-part tariff that has been the focus of this new literature is its non observability. Retailer A does not know the terms of retailer B's contract in stage two, when he must decide whether to accept (W_A^*, F_A^*). This may reflect the reality of many industries. The manufacturer may claim that he will

---

[7] If downstream firms are homogeneous, $P_A^* = P_B^* = P^*$ and Bertrand competition ensures $P = W + r$. Given homogeneous products, linear pricing is sufficient to yield maximal manufacturer profits (achieved by setting $W^* = P^* - r$). If downstream firms are differentiated, $W^* >> m$. The intuition for this can be seen by first assuming a downstream monopoly. In this case, the upstream monopolist would set $W = m$, and the downstream firm would price at $\mathbf{P}^*$. If instead there are imperfectly-competing firms downstream, the competition between these firms would mean that wholesale price of m would result in a retail price below $\mathbf{P}^*$. Thus, given $\partial P_i^R / \partial W_i > 0$, a wholesale price above m is necessary to induce $\mathbf{P}^*$.

[8] See Mathewson and Winter (1984).

[9] This result in shown for the Bertrand game in O'Brien and Shaffer (1992) and McAfee & Schwartz (1991). McAfee and Schwartz (1991) also demonstrate the result for a Cournot game. See also Hart and Tirole (1991).

offer a contract with the optimal terms, ($\mathbf{W}^*$, $\mathbf{F}^*$), to both retailers, but unless each retailer can *observe* that these terms have been offered to the other, each will assume this claim to be false.[10]

It has been suggested that terms of vertical contracts, such as RPM and exclusive territories, are sufficiently public to pass the observability test that two-part tariffs are said to have failed. However, just as the manufacturer cannot be expected to offer two-part tariff contracts not in his interest (hence the importance of observability), the manufacturer cannot be expected to enforce contracts not in his interest to enforce. Even if, upon entering stage two, retailer A is informed about the terms of contract between the manufacturer and retailer B, his contract acceptance decision will depend on his beliefs about whether retailer B will abide by those terms in stage three—i.e., whether they are enforceable.[11] Observability is not sufficient to make a vertical contract into a facilitating device.

The recent literature on vertical contracts has through its focus on observability made some significant theoretical advances at the expense of creating undue optimism about the practical relevance of its findings. This is due to its relative inattention to the basic condition of enforceability necessary to make contracts commitments. The conjecture that contracts, such as RPM and exclusive territories, can solve the observability problem has stimulated new interest in those contracts as facilitating devices, deserving of scrutiny under the law. Whether those conjectures hold up in equilibrium depends on whether those contracts are enforceable.[12]

---

[10] O'Brien and Shaffer (1992 at 301) put it succinctly: "Once observability is dropped, . . . a retailer's pricing decision can no longer be conditioned on his rivals' contracts." See also McAfee and Schwartz (1991 at 2): "contracts with third parties may be unobservable. Due to secret discounts, a firm simply may not know the true input price charged to its rival(s)." A contract between the manufacturer and retailer A that is *not* observable can be renegotiated without retailer B's knowledge. Thus, observable contracts, and unobservable contracts which assume other retailers receive terms that maximize the joint profit of the manufacturer and the other retailer, have been termed "renegotiation proof" (O'Brien and Shaffer (1992)) and "pair-wise proof" (McAfee and Schwartz (1991)), generating "contract" (Cremer and Riordan (1987)) or "simultaneous bargaining" (Horn and Wolinsky (1988)) equilibria.

[11] This introduces the prospect of unilateral deviation. In contrast, the observability assumption is that *bilateral* deviations, involving a retailer and the manufacturer, do not occur.

[12] We use the term enforceable to refer to contracts that are enforced in equilibrium. See definition 2.

III. Strategic Commitment

A vertical contract that is observable and enforceable is here termed a *strategic commitment*. We restrict our attention to sets of bilateral contracts whose terms—other than W and F[13]—are observable, i.e., that cannot be renegotiated by the manufacturer after becoming known to all retailers at the start of stage two. To address whether specific vertical contracts support facilitating-device equilibria requires clarification of conditions under which enforceability can be achieved. There are two such conditions—self-enforcement and external enforcement. The practical relevance of this distinction is that external enforcement typically requires the participation of the courts. To address these considerations in detail, we add a fourth "enforcement" stage to the game set forth in Section II.

In the enforcement stage of the canonical model, as extended here, the courts' interpretation of the law can affect what equilibria are achieved. This stage transpires after retail prices are chosen in stage three but before any customer decisions have been made based on those prices. The assumed effect of enforcement is to bring the deviating retailer's conduct into line with specified contract terms. Thus, if enforcement occurs, the pricing game transpires as indicated by observed contract terms.

We focus on enforcement incentives, setting transactions costs to zero. That is, we assume that the manufacturer's cost of contract enforcement is zero,[14] and that each retailer can costlessly detect and inform the court (external enforcement agencies) of any deviation from terms of any bilateral contract to which the manufacturer is a party. In the canonical game, as extended here, the incentive of a manufacturer or nonsignatory retailer to seek enforcement of a signed bilateral contract in stage four is

---

[13] We assume that W and F are *not* observable to make it possible for a vertical contract to dominate the two-part tariff as a means of extracting surplus from downstream.

[14] Enforcement on the manufacturer's part includes the detection of any deviation from agreed contract terms and the imposition of a sanction that, in combination with the deviation, leaves the deviating retailer worse off than if the deviation had not occurred.

identical to his incentive to make the deviating retailer abide by the contract he has signed. In an alternative, repeat-game setting, a manufacturer or retailer might have an added, reputational incentive to take enforcement action.[15] In such a setting, however, the manufacturer's optimal two-part tariff from Section II would be an equilibrium. To preserve the potential dominance of alternatives to the two-part tariff in extracting downstream surplus, we follow the recent literature in assuming that there are no reputational effects of contract enforcement. In this light, we have the following definition:

Definition 1. A vertical contract is *self-enforcing* if and only if the manufacturer does not benefit from any ex post deviation from its terms.

If a contract is self-enforcing, the retailer knows the manufacturer will not initiate any deviation from its terms and will impose a sanction sufficient to achieve deterrence on any retailer who does.

If the manufacturer can benefit from one retailer's deviation from agreed contract terms at another's expense, the contract is not self-enforcing. The injured retailer must have recourse if the contract is to be enforced. Thus, external enforceability becomes relevant:

Definition 2. A vertical contract is *externally enforceable* if and only if, for any deviation from contract terms that benefits the manufacturer, (a) a retailer recognizes he has been harmed by the deviation and (b) the retailer has standing before a third-party enforcement agency, who can verify that the deviation occurred.[16]

Definition 3. A retailer has *standing* if and only if, in the event of a deviation from the terms of

---

[15] On the role of reputation in ensuring performance, see Coase (1988). More general treatments of the role of reputation include Kreps and Wilson (1982) and Milgrom and Roberts (1982).

[16] Self-enforcement can be defined in terms of external enforcement. That is, one could define self-enforcing contracts as externally enforceable contracts in which the manufacturer has standing before an external enforcement agency, which is exercisable at a sufficiently low cost.

a contract, there exists an enforcement agency with ability and inclination to impose sanctions that, in combination with the deviation, make the deviating parties jointly worse off and, apart from the deviation, makes the injured party (weakly) better off.

Under this definition of external enforceability, standing is necessary and sufficient for the injured retailer to bring the deviation to the enforcement agency's attention. The injured retailer is not made worse off for having exercised his right of standing. The party who deviates from the terms of the contract—the manufacturer or the other retailer in the canonical setting—is worse off after the injured retailer has exercised his right of standing than if the deviation had not occurred. Thus, under external enforceability, deviation from stated contract terms is deterred.

IV. Are Vertical Contracts Strategic Commitments?

Recent suggestions that vertical contracts dominate two-part tariffs as mechanisms to facilitate downstream surplus extraction have focused on RPM and exclusive territory (or closed territory) franchise distribution schemes. Of these, RPM appears to be the more controversial. Currently illegal *per se*, it has been a subject of ongoing debate.[17] In this section, we identify the enforceability conditions that must be met for either of these vertical restraints to be strategic commitments, capable of supporting facilitating-device equilibria.

Under RPM, the vertical contract between manufacturer and retailer specifies a maintained price. At least two types of RPM contracts have been noted in the literature. Under maximum RPM, the retailer agrees under contract to charge no more than the maintained price. Under minimum RPM, he agrees to charge no price below it.

---

[17] For example, see Monsanto Co. v. Spray-Rite Service Corp., 465 U.S. 752 (1984).

Maximum RPM. In the case of maximum RPM, each retailer's contract specifies a maximum retail price and a wholesale price.[18] For example, let retailer A's contract be of the form, $(P_A^\cdot, W_A)$ with $W_A = P_A^\cdot - r$, where r is the marginal cost of retailing the product. The optimal fixed fee in this environment is zero; $F_A = F_B = 0$. We assume that each bilateral maximum RPM contract in the canonical setting is observable; retailer A knows that retailer B has been offered the terms, $(P_B^\cdot, W_B)$ with $W_B = P_B^\cdot - r$. The means by which maximum RPM enables the manufacturer to capture downstream surplus is straight-forward. $P^\cdot$ maximizes the manufacturer and retailers' joint profit, all of which accrues to the manufacturer through payment of the wholesale price. Because the retailer's price equals its marginal cost, there exists no ex post deviation from contract terms that can make the manufacturer better off. Accordingly, we have Proposition 1:

Proposition 1. Maximum RPM is self-enforcing.

Proof: Suppose the manufacturer chooses $P^\cdot = (P_A^\cdot, P_B^\cdot)$ and sets W_i at $P_i^\cdot - r$ and $F_i = 0$ (i = A,B). Given maximum resale prices of $P^\cdot$ and $W = (P_A^\cdot - r, P_B^\cdot - r)$, the manufacturer will choose to enforce the price ceiling because its profits fall as P_i increases above $P_i^\cdot$ (i = A, B). Further, given $W_i = P_i^\cdot - r$, retailer i's profit is increasing in P_i at $P^\cdot$. Thus, retailer i will never charge less than $P_i^\cdot$. Hence, the maximum RPM contract is self-enforcing. ■

Minimum RPM. Each *minimum* RPM contract also specifies a maintained price and a wholesale price, in addition to a fixed fee. Under the assumption that retailer reaction functions are upward sloping, minimum RPM can facilitate extraction of surplus from downstream purchasers. That is, imposing a minimum retail price on retailer A causes retailer B to increase his price (and vice versa). This is desirable

---

[18] For more detailed discussions of how minimum and maximum RPM can be facilitating devices as discussed in the text, see O'Brien and Shaffer (at 305).

from the manufacturer's point of view because, absent minimum RPM, equilibrium prices in a symmetric

Bertrand setting ($\mathbf{P^{Ber}}$) fall short of their joint profit-maximizing levels. It follows that because the

manufacturer can extract all profits accruing at the retail level through wholesale prices and fixed fees,

minimum RPM can make the manufacturer better off. However,

Proposition 2. Minimum RPM is not self-enforcing.

Proof: To show that minimum RPM is not self-enforcing, it is sufficient to show that the manufacturer

and one retailer (retailer A) would benefit from that retailer's decision to undercut the maintained price

($\hat{P}_A$) while the other retailer (retailer B) faces minimum RPM as a binding constraint. Thus, we consider

retailer A's choice of price in stage three (P_A^R) assuming retailer B sets price at the maintained level, $P_B =$

$\hat{P}_B$. A self-enforcing RPM contract is one in which even if retailer A would choose $P_A < \hat{P}_A$ the

manufacturer would be better off with $P_A = \hat{P}_A$. Without loss of generality, assume that $W_A \geq W_B$.

Define $\hat{w}_A$ as the wholesale price at which retailer A's unconstrained optimal price at stage three,

$P_A^R(\hat{w}_A, \hat{w}_B)$, is equal to the maintained level, $\hat{P}_A$. The proof follows in two parts. First, we show that if

$m < W_A < \hat{w}_A$, the manufacturer will choose not to enforce the contract. Second, we show that the

manufacturer will not choose W_A outside this range.

(i) If $\hat{w}_A > W_A > m$, minimum RPM is not self-enforcing. First, since $\partial P_A^R(W_A, \hat{w}_B)/\partial W_A > 0$ (given

standard assumptions of differentiable $Q_A(P_A, P_B)$, unique P_A^R, and $\partial Q_A/\partial P_A < 0$), retailer A would

choose a price below $\hat{P}_A$ in stage three if $W_A < \hat{w}_A$. Second, such a choice would benefit the

manufacturer; $- \partial \pi_m/\partial P_A = (W_A - m) \partial Q_A/\partial P_A + (W_B - m) \partial Q_B/\partial P_B > 0$ because $\partial Q_A/\partial P_A < 0$,

$|\partial Q_A/\partial P_A| > |\partial Q_B/\partial P_A|$, and $W_A \geq W_B$.

(ii) To demonstrate that $\hat{w}_A > W_A > m$, we assume $P_B = \hat{P}_B$, and show that the manufacturer's choice

of W_A is restricted to values that induce retailer A to renege (choose $P_A < \hat{P}_A$). First note that if W_A

$> \hat{w}_A > m$, the manufacturer would be better off lowering W_A. This is because $\partial \pi^*_m / \partial W_A$ $(=$

$(\partial \pi_m / \partial P_A)(\partial P^R_A / \partial W_A)) < 0$ if $P_B = \hat{P}_B$, which self-enforcement implies. It follows that $W_A > \hat{w}_A$ will

never be offered.

Next consider $W_A \leq m$. If $P_A = \hat{P}_A$ and $P_B = \hat{P}_B$, Q_A is independent of W_A (changes in W are

offset by changes in F of the opposite sign and of magnitude equal to Q_A times the change in W); the

manufacturer's profit is the same for all $W_A \leq \hat{w}_A$. However, by (i) we know that if $W_A > m$, the

manufacturer is better off not enforcing compliance (permitting $P_A < \hat{P}_A$). Thus, if the manufacturer

can allow breach, he can earn higher profits by offering $W_A > m$ (with $P_A < \hat{P}_A$) rather than $W_A \leq$

m. (Recall the assumption that B cannot observe W_A or F_A). Thus, $W_A \leq m$ will not be offered.

Similar logic implies that $W_A = \hat{w}_A$ will not be offered since $W_A = \hat{w}_A - \epsilon$ yields the same profits if

enforcement occurs $(P_A = \hat{P}_A)$, but yields higher profits if the manufacturer does not enforce

compliance $(P_A < \hat{P}_A)$. ∎

Corollary. External enforceability is necessary for minimum RPM to be a strategic commitment

(retailer B must have standing in the event of the deviation, $P_A < \hat{P}_A$).

Thus, while maximum and minimum RPM can both qualify as strategic commitments, they require the

support of different enforcement regimes. Aggressive law enforcement may be necessary to prevent

maximum RPM from being used as a facilitating device, but a more passive regime is sufficient to keep

minimum RPM from being used in that way according to the recent theory, as extended here. The courts

could negate the effectiveness of minimum RPM as a facilitating device quite simply—by denying the

harmed retailer standing.

Exclusive Territories. A variety of exclusive or closed territory distribution arrangements have been used to influence conditions under which manufacturers' products are resold.[19] According to Ross (1993

at 224), "*exclusive territorial agreements* permit the retailer to sell only to customers within a designated

geographic area";[20] "*location clauses* permit the retailer to sell to any customer but only from a retailer

outlet in a designated area." Similarly, Tirole (1989) observes that exclusive territories divide the final

market among retailers and that limits on dealer density have a similar restraining effect.

To illustrate how an exclusive territory contract could substitute for the failed two-part tariff as a

facilitating device, consider the use of a location clause that limits retailer density. Suppose the

manufacturer and retailer A agree to a contract making A the sole seller of the good. A two-part tariff

between the manufacturer and retailer A would replicate the vertically integrated solution. This solution

would involve some inefficiency relative to the manufacturer's first-best (i.e, if two-part tariffs were

observable) because the number of retailers would be sub-optimal. Whether exclusive territories are

profitable thus depends on the size of the efficiency loss. In general, if n (>2) retailers would be active

if the two-part tariff were observable, the manufacturer will grant exclusive territories to some m ($<n$) of

them. In a wide class of differentiated-product models, each retailer's Bertrand equilibrium price is

increasing in its "distance" from competing retailers. Reducing the number of retailers from n to m will

thus cause price to rise toward its joint profit-maximizing level.[21]

Under a set of bilateral exclusive territory contracts through which retailers agree to limit the locations

of their outlets (or the customers from whom they solicit sales), each retailer expects to set price above

marginal cost and sell a sufficient quantity to cover the fixed fee that the manufacturer charges. However,

---

[19] For more detailed discussion of how exclusive territories can be facilitating devices, the reader is referred to Hart and Tirole (1991), O'Brien and Shaffer (1992), and McAfee and Schwartz (1991). Hart and Tirole (1991) refer to the type of contract discussed in the text as an "exclusive dealing" arrangement. O'Brien and Shaffer discuss a "closed territory distribution" arrangement that appears to have similar features.

[20] This is termed a "customer restriction" clause by Fox and Sullivan (1989 at 601).

[21] This solution is suggested by Hart and Tirole (1991) and McAfee and Schwartz (1991).

in the canonical environment, it is not in the manufacturer's interest to maintain this expectation after the fixed fee has been paid. At any price set by the incumbent retailer that is above its marginal cost, it is in the manufacturer's interest for another retailer to offer his product to the customers of the incumbent. This other retailer could be new to the manufacturer or already have its own separate exclusive territory contract. In either event:

Proposition 3. Exclusive territory contracts are not self-enforcing.

Proof: The contract that maximizes the manufacturer's profit, given that retailer A alone sells into the territory, consists of $W_A = m$, while retailer A charges the monopoly price, P_M, and pays a fixed fee equal to $(P_M - W_A) Q(P_M, \infty)$.[22] The manufacturer and another retailer, B, can each benefit from sales by retailer B into the territory as long as $P_M > m + r$. More generally, whenever the exclusive territory contract results in $P_A > m + r$, there is some $W_B > m$ at which both retailer B and the manufacturer can be made better off by retailer B's sales into territory reserved for retailer A.∎

Corollary. In order for an exclusive territory to be a strategic commitment, it must be externally enforceable (the harmed retailer must have standing in the event the manufacturer or another retailer sells the manufacturer's product within its territory).

Like minimum RPM, exclusive territory contracts are not self-enforcing. Once the fee is paid, the manufacturer will find it advantageous for one or more additional retailers to begin selling into the incumbent's territory.

To summarize the foregoing discussion, we have the following proposition:

---

[22] Recall the notation, $Q_i = Q_i(P_i, P_j)$.

Proposition 4. External enforceability is necessary for either minimum RPM or exclusive territory

contracts to be strategic commitments.

This has implications for enforcement policy. According to Proposition 4, under recent theories of

vertical restraints as facilitating devices, a policy of non-intervention by the courts (e.g., denying retailers

standing when others invade their territory) is sufficient to prevent vertical restraints from being used as

facilitating devices. Vigorous law enforcement programs such as per se bans on RPM and exclusive

territories are not required.

V.   Evidence of Strategic Commitment

Our analysis has focused thus far on the enforceability requirements of strategic commitment. To be

facilitating devices, both minimum RPM and exclusive territory contracts must be externally enforceable.

Unlike maximum RPM, they have the (socially) desirable property that passive non-enforcement regimes

are sufficient to prevent their use as facilitating devices under recent theories of vertical restraints. In this

section, we consider whether such regimes have characterized U.S. law. We turn to the statute and case

law for this purpose. Because RPM has been per se illegal since 1975,[23] we consider the legal

environment surrounding RPM before that time. In the case of exclusive territories, which are judged

under a rule of reason standard, we rely upon more recent evidence.

A. Minimum Resale Price Maintenance

The years between 1937 and 1975 were the period of greatest legal protection of minimum RPM. If

RPM has ever had value as a strategic commitment, it would have been during this period. The Miller-

---

[23] Under the McGuire Act, RPM was permitted if expressly authorized by state law. Outside of this exception, which was repealed in 1975, RPM has been per se illegal under *Dr. Miles* since 1911. Our discussion of the statutory history of RPM derives from Ippolito and Overstreet (1992) and Overstreet (1983).

Tydings Act of 1937 enabled states to permit use of RPM, which under the Sherman Act was otherwise per se illegal. State laws under which RPM was legal were initially interpreted as requiring that every retailer in the state adhere to any RPM contract between a manufacturer and any other retailer doing business in that state.[24] That is, state law was interpreted as holding "non-signers" to terms of signed bilateral RPM contracts. Congress in 1952 responded to the Supreme Court's 1951 decision[25] against this interpretation of existing statute by passing the McGuire Act, making explicit its intention that states be allowed to pass laws extending the terms of bilateral RPM contracts to non-signers. Some of the state "fair trade" laws passed in response had non-signer provisions while others did not.[26] The Miller-Tydings Act was repealed in 1975.

Clearly, statutes that supported the legality of RPM between 1937 and 1975 went a long way toward supporting the *observability* of RPM. A retailer could in most states be assured that if he had an RPM clause in his bilateral contract with a manufacturer, other retailers operating in that state would have the clause as well. The exception is the individual retailer operating in a state whose RPM statute did not have a non-signer provision after 1951.

These same statutes, however, did not provide for *external enforceability* of RPM. Our review of the case law from that time has uncovered no evidence of the courts' willingness to enforce RPM contracts absent evidence that enforcement would benefit the manufacturer ex post. This leads us to conclude that RPM contracts, though observable, were not externally enforceable.

In reaching this empirical finding about the enforceability of minimum RPM, we searched the case law

---

[24] Of the 48 states, only Missouri, Texas and Vermont never legalized RPM.

[25] *Schwegmann Bros. v. Calvert Distillers Corp.*, 341 U.S. 384 (1951) held that the Miller-Tydings Act did not extend antitrust immunity to enforcement of RPM against non-signers.

[26] The exact number of states allowing non-signer provisions varied over the years. In 1970 for example, 19 states had 'fair trade' laws permitting RPM, but not extending it to non-signers, 17 states had 'fair trade' laws which included non-signer provisions, and 14 states did not permit RPM.

for instances in which an injured retailer successfully brought suit without the manufacturer's endorsement. No such cases were found. To learn why such evidence may not exist, we investigated the conditions under which standing could have been achieved. The two most likely avenues through which an injured retailer could have achieved standing between 1937 and 1975 were under contract law and under state fair trade statute. The discussion of these two avenues that follows suggests why an injured retailer may have been unable to achieve standing through those avenues.

Under contract law, we considered the possibility that an injured retailer would sue either the manufacturer or the other retailer for breach. The injured retailer's problem in suing for breach of contract is that he is not a signatory to the bilateral RPM contract from which another retailer has deviated. To gain standing, the injured retailer must thus convince the court that he is a "third-party beneficiary" of the contract. U.S. law at the time of the passage of the Miller-Tydings Act, as reflected in § 133 of the *First Restatement, Contracts* (1932), recognized the rights of "donee" or gift-receiving, third-party beneficiaries.[27] The standard example of a third party as donee beneficiary is the case where a parent contracts with a painter to paint a son's house. The son would have standing to sue the painter for breach if the house were not painted. The situation of an injured retailer in the case of minimum RPM does not appear to fit this case, and hence does not appear to have qualified the retailer to sue as a third-party beneficiary at the time the Miller-Tydings Act was passed.

The standard under which third-party beneficiaries are recognized has become more liberal over time. It is conceivable that this standard became sufficiently liberal that sometime before the Miller-Tydings Act was repealed in 1975 a retailer injured by another's deviation from RPM contract terms may have gained standing. Even so, our reading of the literature on the more contemporary legal standard suggests to us

---

[27] See Calamari and Perillo, Contracts, 691.

that it would have been very difficult for an injured retailer to gain standing even as late as 1975. Of the more liberal circumstances cited in the *Second Restatement, Contracts* (1982), that of the "intended beneficiary" seems to come closest to that of the injured retailer in the case of minimum RPM.[28] However, the injured party's circumstance in the event of non-enforcement of an RPM contract seems better illustrated by examples offered in the Second Restatement of circumstances under which the third party does *not* have standing to sue. In one such example, A and B have a contract to make improvements to A's land, which would benefit C.[29] In another, automaker C benefits from A's contract to buy a car from auto dealer B. In neither example does C have standing.[30]

One fairly recent case seems to illustrate the principle. In *Staten Island Rustproofing V. Ziebart Rustproofing* (U.S.D.C., EDNY, #85-C-1985), the plaintiff, a franchisee of the defendant, claimed that the defendant allowed another (geographically proximate) franchisee to violate terms of its contract with the defendant. The breach consisted of the other franchisee failing to operate in accordance with uniform standards, thereby lowering the reputation of Ziebart's rustproofing business throughout the metropolitan area, and injuring plaintiff.

As emphasized in the recent literature, all retailers can be harmed by a single retailer's decision to charge less than the manufacturer's contractually-maintained price. Similar harms have arisen in cases where retailers have chosen to provide less than the contractually-specified level of service. In *Staten Island Rustproofing*, such a contract violation led the retailer to bring suit against its supplier. The contract allegedly breached was between the manufacturer and another retailer. The court held that Staten Island Rustproofing did not have any right to relief because it was not a signatory of the contract in question, nor

---

[28] "Intended beneficiaries" expands the donee class to include individuals whom the promisee "intended to benefit." Under this standard, the third party beneficiary must show that recognition of contractual rights is "appropriate to effectuate the intention of the parties." See Second Restatement, § 302.

[29] § 302, illustration 16.

[30] § 302, illustration 17.

did it have standing as an incidental beneficiary. This holding suggests that, by contemporary legal standards, one retailer injured by another's breach of an RPM contract would have difficulty gaining standing in an RPM-related action at contract law. It explains our difficulty identifying past cases in which any retailer sought relief in response to harm caused by another's breach of its contract with the manufacturer to adhere to a maintained price; cases in which RPM contracts were enforced at contract law are either few or do not exist.

We have, however, found ample evidence of efforts to enforce RPM contracts through the application of statutory Fair Trade laws. Some of these cases were brought by manufacturers and some were brought by injured retailers.[31] In cases brought between 1937 and 1975, where manufacturers were found successfully to have brought suit to prevent their retailers from charging less than the maintained price, the manufacturer's burden was to demonstrate that it had taken actions directed toward enforcement of the maintained price. The nature of this burden is made clear in *General Electric v. R.H. Macy & Co.* 103, N.Y.S.2d 440 (S. Ct. 1951) in which the manufacturer's burden was to demonstrate that it monitored the prices charged in the market, enforced those prices (through "repeated legal action if necessary") and maintained a "continued and sustained" enforcement program.[32] The evidence is that injured retailers attempting to obtain price relief against rival retailers' charging less the maintained price faced a similar burden. For example, in *Rothbaum v. R.H. Macy Co, Inc.*, 115 N.Y.S.2d 197 (Sup. Ct. App. Div. 1952), a retail druggist was able to prevent price cutting by a rival because it was shown that the manufacturer of the Fair-Traded item generally enforced the maintained price. Conversely, in *Pordes v. Lythe*, 137 N.Y.S.2d 422 (S.Ct. 1955), the court found that Pordes (another retail druggist) was not entitled to an

---

[31] Leading cases involving manufacturers bringing suit to prevent retailers from charging below the maintained price include *General Electric Co. v. R.H. Macy & Co.*, 103 N.Y.S.2d 440 (S.Ct. 1951), *General Electric Co. v. Hess Bros., Inc.*, 155 F. Supp. 57 (E.D. Pa. 1957), *Esterbrook Pen Co., v San Juan F. Vilarano 5 Y 10, Inc.*, 144 F Supp. 309 (D.P.R. 1956), *Sunbeam Corp. v. Marcus*, 105 F. Supp. 39 (S.D.N.Y. 1952).

[32] This case has been described as "perhaps the leading case on the subject" (in *General Electric Company v. Hess Brothers, Inc.* 155 F. Supp. 57), and these principles have been broadly applied.

injunction against a price cutter because the manufacturer of the product in question had not enforced the maintained price. The implication is that if the manufacturer did *not* benefit from enforcement of the RPM contract, the injured retailer could not successfully sue under state Fair Trade laws. Put differently, the theories under which courts were willing to enforce minimum RPM under state statute are not consistent with external enforceability of minimum RPM.

B. Exclusive Territories

One might anticipate that a manufacturer would encounter less difficulty using exclusive territories as a strategic commitment device. An exclusive territory contract that restricts a manufacturer from selling into a given retailer's territory, either directly or through an intermediary, would not have the initial observability problems of RPM. The manufacturer restriction clause, in effect, writes the locational terms of all retailer's contracts into each bilateral contract that the manufacturer signs. At issue is whether the courts have been willing to enforce this manufacturer restriction clause. If so, exclusive territories contracts with manufacturer restriction clauses in place would meet conditions of observability and (ex post) enforceability necessary to make them strategic commitments.

The evidence from the case law is that exclusive territory contracts with manufacturer restriction clauses are, indeed, externally enforceable. For example, in *Bausch & Lomb v. Bressler and Sonomed Technology, Inc.*, 977 F.2d 770 (2d Cir. 1992), the distributor (Bausch & Lomb) sued a manufacturer of ophthalmic diagnostic instruments for wrongful termination and for breaching their agreement by selling products into the distributor's territory. The court held in plaintiff's favor, finding that the parties' contract had involved payment of a fixed fee in exchange for "exclusive distribution rights" and was violated by the defendant's act of selling into plaintiff's territory. Damages involved refund of the fixed fee minus profits previously earned by defendant under the contract. As *Bausch & Lomb* indicates, exclusive territory contracts with manufacturer restriction clauses are externally enforceable and can thus meet both observability conditions necessary to make them strategic commitments.[33]

However, the exclusive territory contract in *Bausch & Lomb* may be atypical. More common among the "exclusive territory" cases we were able to locate were cases involving contracts that did *not* have manufacturer restriction clauses.[34] Through such contracts, each retailer agrees to limit his sales to an assigned territory (or location or set of customers). But the manufacture does not agree to restrict sales of the product through other outlets into that territory. The contract debated in *Continental T.V., Inc. v. GTE Sylvania Inc.*, 433 U.S. 36 (1977), which is widely cited among exclusive territory cases, serves to illustrate.[35] As noted by the *Sylvania* court, "Sylvania retained sole discretion to increase the number of retailers in an area." Sylvania's contract with its distributors granted them territories and restricted them to those territories. Continental brought suit against Sylvania after Sylvania gave another distributor the right to sell its product from a location one mile away from Continental's store. Sylvania's contractual right to introduce new distributors into Continental's territory was ultimately recognized by the court.

Most of the exclusive territory cases that we found in the Federal case law resemble *Sylvania* in prohibiting the retailer from selling outside its territory, while placing no explicit complementary

---

[33] In *Exercycle of Michigan v. B. Wayson and Hales & Hearty, Inc.*, 341 F.2d 335 (7th Cir. 1965), the court also defended a distributor as plaintiff against sales by another into its territory. That case however, did *not* involve enforcement of a manufacturer restriction clause. One distributor (Exercycle of Michigan) sued another (Wayson) for selling into the territory that the manufacturer had granted it, claiming breach of contract and malicious interference. The court observed that defendant Wayson had been restricted from selling outside its own territory and that it had been reminded by the manufacturer (after plaintiff complained). Thus, the case involved enforcement of a distributor restriction clause—not a manufacturer restriction clause—in the presence of evidence that the manufacturer was actively seeking to enforce it. As other cases noted in the text demonstrate, the courts have not enforced distributor restriction clauses in response to distributor complaints without the manufacturer's cooperation.

[34] We are aware of no evidence that this absence of manufacturer restriction clauses responds to any legal prohibition placed on manufacturers by the courts.

[35] In *Sylvania*, the Supreme court reversed *Schwinn* and upheld the use of rule of reason analysis in cases involving nonprice vertical restraint.

restrictions on the manufacturer's downstream locational decisions.[36] Even those cases that have been characterized as involving enforcement of manufacturer restriction clauses by the court turn out, upon closer inspection, to involve enforcement of the manufacturer's right to sell to one retailer at another's expense.[37]

Of the contracts that give rise to the exclusive territories outcome, we find that only those contracts that explicitly restrict the manufacturer's right to sell into the retailer's designated territory are externally enforcing. The courts have been unwilling to read such a restriction into the retailer's contract where it has not been made explicit. Thus, contracts that lack the manufacturer restriction clauses face the same enforceability problems as minimum RPM. They are not strategic commitments capable of supporting facilitating-device equilibria, and consequently must serve some other purpose, where observed.

VI. Discussion

Recent treatments of vertical contracts as facilitating devices have focused on their observability properties and have assumed they will be enforced. As we have shown, enforcement of the most widely discussed vertical contracts requires court participation. The recent literature on vertical contracts is thus shown to have powerful implications for optimal legal rules. The implication is that, in order to keep these

---

[36] For example, *Valley Liquors v. Renfield Importers, Ltd.*, 822 F.2d 656 (7th Cir. 1987), upheld the manufacturer's right to re-allocate "exclusive" territories among distributors. As is typical of cases of this type, the distributor (Valley) brought suit under section 1 of the Sherman Act and state law (breach of distributor agreement).

[37] For example, the district court in *United States v. White Motor Co.*, 194 F. Supp. 562, 578 (N.D. Ohio 1961), distinguishes two types of exclusive territory agreements ("conflicting definitions") which corresponds to our distinction between clauses that restrict distributors only and those that restrict manufacturers as well. The court found that restrictions of the second type have generally been upheld. However, even the cases cited as falling into this category are, upon closer examination, cases in which the court enforced the manufacturer's right to place one distributor in territory previously reserved for another (the plaintiff). For example, *Schwing Motor Co v. Hudson Sales Co.*, 239 F.2d 176 (4th Cir. 1956) and *Packard Motor Car Co. v. Webster Motor Car Co.*, 243 F.2d 418 (D.C. Cir. 1957), are cited as falling into this second category, but actually address the manufacturer's right to not renew a distributor's exclusive territory agreement at its annual expiration date—a right the court upheld. The dispute in *White*, like that in *Sylvania* fell into the first category.

contracts from being used as facilitating devices, it is sufficient for courts to apply a legal rule which defers to the manufacturer's short-term interest. In the case of minimum RPM, this means denying standing to retailers injured by other retailers' price-cutting behavior if the manufacturer has made no effort to prevent it. In the case of exclusive territories, it means not enforcing the manufacturer restriction clause.

Our reading of the case law is that the courts have operated as prescribed by the recent theory with respect to RPM (before the Miller-Tydings Act was repealed), but not with respect to exclusive territory contracts. While many exclusive territory contracts do *not* have a manufacturer restriction clause, when it is present this clause is enforced by the courts. We find even greater tension between state statutes and recent theory. For example, numerous states *require* exclusive territories to be assigned in the distribution of beer.[38] To the extent these laws limit manufacturers' short-term discretion in making territorial assignments, they are social welfare-reducing under the theory extended here.

In general, if the recent theory of vertical contracts as facilitating devices is of any practical relevance, current legal rules may be suboptimal from a social welfare perspective. Under the recent theory, it is possible to make minimum RPM and exclusive territory contracts lawful at both the state and Federal levels without any harm to the social welfare, provided that the courts defer to the manufacturer's short-turn interest when making enforcement decisions.

While our extension of the recent literature on vertical restraints has the foregoing implications for legal rulemaking, it raises questions about the practical relevance of the related theory. Minimum RPM, when legal, did not meet enforceability conditions necessary to make it a strategic commitment and, consequently, a facilitating device. With similar implication, many exclusive territory contracts have been

---

[38] "The alcoholic beverage control laws of 30 states (i.e., 60% of the states) mandate (i.e., require) exclusive territories and prohibit wholesaler sales outside the brewer-assigned territories." *Memorandum and Order: New York v. Anheuser-Busch, Inc.*, 811 F. Supp. 848 (E.D.N.Y. 1993).

written without manufacturer restriction clauses, leaving enforcement to the manufacturer's discretion. Yet despite these features, viable minimum RPM and exclusive territory arrangements are observed in the world. This could not happen in the canonical environment and suggests that premises of the related theory are, from a practical standpoint, flawed.

This suggests alternative explanations of these vertical restraints may be in order. In particular, we note that prominent "efficiency" explanations of vertical restraints are often modeled in repeat-game contexts, where reputation effects mitigate the incentive for opportunistic behavior. On the other hand, even if we disregard efficiency explanations, in a repeat game, reputation effects may prevent the kind of opportunism problems that make the first best two-part tariff contract unsupportable. For example, our observation that exclusive territory contracts frequently only restrict the retailer suggests that potential loss of reputation constrains the manufacturer from acting opportunistically. Once we allow for reputation effects, however, two-part tariff may dominate other vertical restraints as means of extracting surplus from downstream. In both the repeat game and static game, we find that the facilitating device view of minimum RPM and exclusive territory contracts that do not explicitly constrain the manufacturer is flawed.

Finally, the enforceability dimension of strategic commitment that we have developed has relevance beyond the canonical environment that has been our focus. As strategic commitment devices, contracts can be powerful tools. Their potential as facilitating devices is yet to be fully explored by economists. However, it is clear from the early contributions to the broader literature on contracts as facilitating devices that enforceability issues will arise that must be addressed before its practical relevance can be known. Some of the contributions to this broader literature on vertical contracts as facilitating devices have applied a result due to Cooper (1986) that was exploited in Section II. Specifically, Cooper showed that starting from an equilibrium in which differentiated firms compete on the basis of price (i.e., the Bertrand equilibrium), a firm's unilateral price increase is profitable. The problem with such an increase is that the increase must be communicated to one's rivals, and it is difficult to make it observable or enforceable. Several papers have suggested that there are contractual means of accomplishing this objective. As we discuss, in each case it is unclear how the proposed solution makes the offer either observable or enforceable.

Cooper (1986) suggested that instituting a most-favored nation (MFN) clause can alter a retailer's reaction function, enabling him to increase profits by raising the equilibrium level of prices.[39] In Cooper's model, retailers sell in each of two periods. Before making any sales, each can announce a policy under which it will rebate the price difference to its first-period customers if its second-period price is less than its first-period price. Suppose retailer A announces such a policy. The direct effect is to alter his second-period reaction in the neighborhood of the first-period price. This increases retailer B's optimal second-period price. That retailer A profits from retailer B's price increase gives it an incentive to increase its first-period price, given an MFN clause. Announcement of an MFN clause thus raises the prices charged by both retailers.

It would seem that an announced MFN contract is readily enforceable; if customer A found out that customer B received a lower price, he would seem to have standing to sue the retailer for the price differential. However, other conditions for enforceability are less clear. That is, customer A has no incentive to reveal his price to customer B (and may have a disincentive if customer B is a competitor). Further, A's price may not be demonstrable to the court. Moreover, the conditions for ex-ante observability may well be lacking; although a retailer may announce a policy of MFN, his rival needs to know that the contracts the retailer signs actually contains the clause.

---

[39] For additional discussions of the facilitating-device uses of MFN clauses, see Grether and Plott (1984), Holt and Scheffman (1987), Cooper (1986), Salop (1986), and Neilsen and Winter (1993). On other uses of the MFN clause, see Butz (1990) and P'ng (1991).

Cooper seems aware of these problems. He cites use of MFN in the turbine industry and notes that suppliers of turbines were able to publicly announce their MFN policies.[40] Further, he contends that the manufacturers allowed customers to check sales records for any relevant price cut. While the manufacturer would like to convince first-period customers that such records would be accurate, his incentive changes in the second period. That is, the agreement to reveal price is not self-enforcing (nor would it appear to be externally enforceable). From a practical standpoint, this implies that neither the manufacturer nor second-period customers have the incentive to maintain or reveal accurate records.

Turning to more recent illustrations of the importance of enforceability in determining what facilitating-device equilibria can be achieved, Shaffer (1991) considers an environment in which multiple manufacturers produce a homogeneous good and compete for the business of retailer duopolists, so that all rents eventually accrue downstream. In this environment, an observable two-part tariff characterized by $W > m$ and $F < 0$ (i.e., the manufacturer pays the retailer a fixed fee) can enable the retailer to commit to a higher retail price. Shaffer suggests such a contract may be unobservable and proposes that minimum RPM may be a superior rent-extraction device. He shows that if a manufacturer can communicate to retailers that it will enforce a specific maintained price (greater than P^{Ber}) on retailer A, retailer B will assume that retailer A will charge this price. The empirical relevance of this result is limited, however, by previously stated findings. The minimum RPM contract set forth by Shaffer as a means of extracting surplus from upstream is not externally enforceable and is thus not a strategic commitment capable of supporting the equilibrium proposed. Not only does Shaffer's minimum RPM contract lack the benefit of non-signer laws (casting doubt on the observability), but lacking a contract with either party to the breached bilateral minimum RPM contract, the injured retailer's standing to enforce that contract is remote.

---

[40] Neilson and Winter (1993) show that under standard demand conditions, including those assumed here, it is not an equilibrium for both suppliers to use MFN clauses. For this reason, the use of MFN clauses by both suppliers of turbines does not fit Cooper's model.

A final example is the suggestion by Ordover, Salop and Saloner (1991) that a retailer can through vertical integration strategically commit its supplier (a duopolist) to charge a higher price to its rival, raising the equilibrium wholesale price faced by that rival above m. This in turn induces the rival to increase its price above P^{Ber}. Questions about this strategic commitment assumption are raised by Reiffen (1992) and Hart and Tirole (1991). Of particular interest here, vertical integration is not sufficient to support an equilibrium price above P^{Ber} because an announced plan by the acquired upstream firm to charge a higher wholesale price after the merger is not enforceable. No one with an incentive to challenge deviation from the announced plan has legal standing to do so. The integrated firm would have an incentive to lower its wholesale price below the announced level and the equilibrium, P^{Ber}, would be achieved.

To summarize, the idea that firms may take actions to alter their future reactions (i.e., make commitments) is not limited to the canonical setting of Section II. When an action involves acquisition of productive assets with low salvage value (as in Spence (1977)), its strategic commitment value is clear. When the action is contractual, however, the question of whether it serves as a strategic commitment is inevitably linked to the enforcement regime.[41] This paper's development of the enforceability aspect of strategic commitment sheds light on conditions that must be met for contracts to support facilitating-device equilibria in a wide range of settings.

VII. Conclusion

A significant portion of modern industrial organization theory is concerned with strategic commitment. Using models based on strategic commitment has enabled recent theorists to identify equilibria in which various actions have adverse welfare consequences. This paper has advanced the theory in both a general

---

[41] Thus, questions raised here about the usefulness of contracts as strategic commitments extend to the usefulness of intra-firm contracts as means of committing to price or quantity, as proposed by Fershtman and Judd (1987). For a discussion of the practical relevance of intra-firm contracts as in this context, see Lott and Opler (1993).

and a specific context. We provide structure to the concept of strategic commitment by setting out conditions under which facilitating-device equilibria can be supported by a firm's actions, particularly contractual ones. A contract is a strategic commitment if it affects the incentives of the manufacturer and communicates this change in incentives to relevant third parties. In many contexts, whether these conditions are met depends on the legal environment. The condition of external enforceability, emphasized here, relates the legal status of a contract to its commitment value. As we have shown, external enforceability is a necessary condition for some of the most widely discussed vertical contracts to have strategic commitment value. By developing the enforceability conditions necessary to strategic commitment, we suggest an avenue through which the practical relevance of the emerging literature on contracts as facilitating devices may be explored.

To illustrate, we have examined legal environments within which minimum RPM and exclusive territory contracts have been enforced. Contrary to conjectures made in the recent literature, the evidence is that RPM has not met the enforceability conditions necessary for it to be a strategic commitment. Nor in many instances have the exclusive territory contracts brought before the courts. The evidence is that these vertical contracts have not met conditions necessary to support their use as facilitating devices in equilibrium.

This paper has uncovered a harmony between the policy implications of the two sides of the vertical restraint debate. Some of those who view vertical restraints as facilitating devices base their analysis on an assumption that the restraints are designed to limit manufacturers' abilities to behave opportunistically toward their retailers. Conversely, those who view vertical restraints as efficiency-enhancing tend to regard manufacturer discretion in the short run as necessary to protect product quality. From a policy perspective, court holdings that follow a legal rule allowing manufacturers maximum discretion in matters such as terminating dealers and locating additional dealers are consistent with the desire to uphold a social welfare standard under either view of the restraints.

References

Blechman, "Conscious Parallelism, Signalling and Facilitating Devices: The Problem of Tacit Collusion Under the Antitrust Laws," *N.Y.L. School L. Rev. 24* (1979) 881.

Butz, David A., "Durable-Good Monopoly and Best-Price Provisions," *American Economic Review* 80 (1990) 1062-75.

Calamari, John D. and Joseph M. Perillo, *Contracts* (3d ed.), West Publishing, 1987.

Coase, Ronald "The Nature of the Firm: Influence," *Journal of Law and Economics and Organization* 4 (1988), 33-47.

Cooper, Thomas P. "Most Favored Nation Pricing and Tacit Collusion," *Rand Journal of Economics* 17 (1986), 377-88.

Cremer, Jacques and Michael H. Riordan, "On Governing Multilateral Transactions with Bilateral Contracts," *Rand Journal of Economics* 18 (1987) 436-51.

Fershtman, Chaim and Kenneth L. Judd "Equilibrium Incentives in Oligopoly," *American Economic Review* 77 (1987) 927-940

Fox, Eleanor M. and Lawrence A. Sullivan, *Cases and Materials on Antitrust*, West Publishing Co. (1989).

Grether, D. M. and Charles R. Plott "The Effects of Market Practices in Oligopolistic Markets: An Experimental Examination of the Ethyl Case," *Economic Inquiry* 22 (1984), 479-528.

Kreps, David and Robert Wilson "Reputation and Imperfect Information," *Journal of Economic Theory* 27 (1982) 253-79.

Hart, Oliver and Jean Tirole, "Vertical Integration and Market Foreclosure," *Brookings Papers on Economic Activity 1990*, 205-276.

Holt, Charles A. and David T. Scheffman "Facilitating Practices: the Effects of Advance Notice and Best-Price Provisions," *Rand Journal of Economics*, 18 (1987) 187-197.

Horn, Henrick and Asher Wolinsky "Bilateral Monopoly and the Incentives for Mergers," *Rand Journal of Economics*, 19 (1988) 408-19.

Ippolito, Pauline M. and Thomas R. Overstreet, *Resale Price Maintenance: An Economic Study of the FTC's Case Against the Corning Glass Works*, 1993, Federal Trade Commission, Washington, DC.

Klein, Benjamin and Kevin M. Murphy, "Vertical Restraints as Contract Enforcement Mechanisms," *Journal of Law and Economics* 31 (1988), 265-97.

Lott, John and Timothy Opler, "Testing Whether Predatory Commitments are Credible," mimeo. (1992).

Mathewson, G. Frank and Ralph A. Winter, "An Economic Theory of Vertical Restraints," *Rand Journal of Economics* 15 (1984), 27-38.

Mathewson, G. Frank and Ralph A. Winter, "The Competitive Effects of Vertical Agreements: Comment," *American Economic Review* 77 (1987), 1057-1062.

McAfee, R. Preston and Marius Schwartz, "Two-Part Tariffs to Competing Firms: Destructive Recontracting, Nondiscrimination, and Exclusivity," EAG Discussion Paper 91-1, U.S. Department of Justice, January 1991 (forthcoming, *American Economic Review*).

Milgrom, Paul and John Roberts "Predation, Reputation, and Entry Deterrence," *Journal of Economic Theory* 27 (1982) 280-312.

Neilson, William and Harold Winter, "Bilateral Most-Favored-Customer Pricing and Collusion," *Rand Journal of Economics* 24 (1993) 147-55.

O'Brien, Daniel P. and Greg Shaffer, "Vertical Control with Bilateral Contracts," *Rand Journal of Economics* 23 (1992), 299-308.

Ordover, Janusz, Steven C. Salop and Garth Saloner "Equilibrium Vertical Foreclosure," *American Economic Review* 80 (1990), 127-42.

Overstreet, Thomas R. *Resale Price Maintenance: Economic Theories and Empirical Evidence*, November 1983, Federal Trade Commission, Washington, DC,.

Pashigian, Peter, "Limit Price and the Market Share of the Leading Firm," *Journal of Industrial Economics* 16, (1968), 165-77.

P'ng, Ivan, "Most-Favored-Customer Protection Versus Price Discrimination Over Time," *Journal of Political Economy* 99 (1991), 1010-23.

Reiffen, David A. "Equilibrium Vertical Foreclosure Comment," *American Economic Review* 80 (1990), 694-7.

Rey, Patrick and Jean Tirole, "The Logic of Vertical Restraints," 76 *American Economic Review* 76 (1986), 921-939.

Restatement and Restatement (Second) of Contracts (1934 and 1982).

Ross, Stephen F., *Principles of Antitrust Law* (1993).

Salop, Steven C. "Practices that (Credibly) Facilitate Oligopoly Coordination," in Stiglitz and Mathewson, eds. *New Developments in the Analysis of Market Structure* (1986).

Shaffer, Greg, "Slotting Allowances and Resale Price Maintenance: A Comparison of Facilitating Practices," *Rand Journal of Economics* 22 (Spring, 1991), 120-35.

Spence, A. Michael, "Entry, Capacity, Investment and Oligopoly Pricing," *Bell Journal of Economics and Management* 8 (1977) 534-44.

Stigler, George, *The Organization of Industry*, Richard D. Irwin, Inc. (1968).

Sylos-Labini, Paolo, *Oligopoly and Technical Progress*, Cambridge University Press (1962).

Telser, Lester, "Why Should Manufacturers Want Fair Trade?," *Journal of Law and Economics* 3 (1960), 86-105.

Tirole, Jean, *The Theory of Industrial Organization*, MIT Press (1989).

Whinston, Michael, "Tying, Foreclosure, and Exclusion," *American Economic Review*, 80 (1990), 837-59.

www.ingramcontent.com/pod-product-compliance
Lightning Source LLC
Chambersburg PA
CBHW081315180526
45170CB00007B/2719